The Personality Development of a Serial Killer

-A Psychoanalytic Analysis of Jeffrey Dahmer-

BA.pth. Paula Ciocirlau

Author: BA.pth. Paula Ciocirlau

Table of contents

Abstract

Jeffrey Dahmer's mother was disturbed during her entire pregnancy and consequently she was given massive amounts of drugs such as barbiturates and phenobarbital. Jeffrey was a happy kid, born with a fundamental problem with his foot, which has been successfully operated, and later on due to a hernia he has developed, he showed castration anxiety. The marriage of his parents was heated with violent arguments. By the time he finished high school, Jeffrey has developed an alcoholic problem. Later on, he was diagnosed with borderline personality disorder, schizotypal personality disorder, psychotic disorder and autism although these have not been the main reason to commit crimes. Most of his life he was plagued by feelings of loneliness and isolation which made him long for a permanent companion.

Keywords: Jeffrey Dahmer, necrophilia, sexual aggression, serial sexual homicide, antisocial behaviour, multiple diagnoses, personality development

Introduction

The rapidly increase concern about violence and crime in the industrialized world has undeniably led to escalating fears, consequently creating an intimidation climate. To approach and alleviate this menace, it requires an understanding of its causes and, thus, entails advancement in the knowledge as wells as an understanding of the problems. Ironically much remedial activity in situations with victims of the offense only facilitates for treatment rather prevention. It is therefore hoped that exploring the issue, concerning the offender, the insight which could eventually enhance preventative work may come to light: comprehending perpetrator violence can significantly contribute to lowered victimization coupled with improved rehabilitation.

Psychoanalytic theory can increase understanding of some of the functions and origins of violent and criminal behaviours of individuals. Notably, its theory can be used to improve the knowledge of atrocious, killers, and sexually coercive fantasies alongside the acts of those offending in such manner.

Even in the availability of severe psychopathology in serial killers, the real reasons for committing serial killings are not instantly overtly apparent or obvious, so analysis of the underlying personality and psychopathology of the murderer is of relevant in understanding the repetitive, compulsive drive to murder. Human behaviour is essential, and it is powerfully impacted by the forces (elements) outside of awareness;

therefore, these motivations and meanings while always not instantly visible are decipherable by internalizing meanings of experiences and unconscious (Tithecott, 1999). This way, the psychoanalytic theory provides a mechanism to question what elements (factors) motivate a person to become a killer in a sexually abhorrent manner. This Bachelor thesis aims to do this by leveraging on both exploratory and descriptive research utilizing the existing literature and then setting forth the outcome.

This Bachelor thesis aims to look at what might have influenced the crimes of the most heinous crime, sexually motivated killer of all time, Jeffrey Dahmer, the son of Joyce and Lionel Dahmer, which premeditatedly has tortured and murdered seventeen men, committing acts of necrophilia. When dealing with Dahmer, we have to bear in mind the following facts that will be used in the course of the Bachelor thesis:

- *Antisocial behaviour.* As referred to in the literature, antisocial behaviour relates to any practice reflecting on violations of social acts or norms negatively towards others. Generally, antisocial acts cause pain, suffering and distress to the victims. Jeffrey certainly meets criteria for the antisocial personality disorder. He lured all his victims by way of disarming them and making them feel like he could be trusted, before brutally violating their trust and performing his criminal acts on them.

- *Influence of alcohol*: Research indicates that most necrophiliacs are perpetrated under the influence of alcohol when acted upon their fantasies with Jeffrey Dahmer being the most known case. They tend to be become hostile and aggressive while drinking alcohol, as well as committing most of the serial sexual homicides while under the influence of alcohol.

- *Developmental stages*: Jeffrey's homosexuality is closely associated with his dad's absence and feminine dominance in his life. Across developmental stages, a person encounters conflicts, and if those are not well resolved, a fixation occurs. During these stages, the id, the ego, and the superego aspects of personality are involved. Jeffrey under-indulgence contributed to his aggressive oral character; since this was extreme Jeffrey showed dominance and cruel behaviour. The subject never learned to create healthy relationships with his peers. He had a failed Oedipus complex since he never bonded well with his mother, Joyce and thus, he was focused on getting pleasure by fully controlling other people.

- *Question of legal sanity*: Due to of the nature of his gruesome crimes, his mental condition was questioned as it is hard to imagine anybody performing such crimes unless they are criminally insane. By daily definition, he might very likely be insane but by legal standard he was deemed sane to stand trial, the reason being him trying to cover up his crimes, which is strong evidence that he could tell wrong from right.

1. Jeffrey Dahmer's life story from his father's viewpoint

Reconstructing Jeffrey Dahmer's life events, with a special focus on his childhood, according to psychoanalytic theories, it is a very important link to his diagnostics and their development.

Jeffrey Dahmer was the first son of Joyce and Lionel Dahmer, born in

Milwaukee, Wisconsin on May 21, 1960. Joyce's pregnancy was a hard one. During the first part of the pregnancy, Joyce Dahmer began to suffer from morning nausea, which is a very normal thing to experience in the first month of pregnancy, but as the time went by, Joyce began to experience the nausea and even vomiting daily. She became so weak; she eventually had to quit her job (Dahmer, 1994, p. 31). In the time she was home, Joyce felt neither physically nor emotionally good. Not long since she decided to stay home, she became irritated and nervous. The noise and cooking smell of the neighbours below, which according to Lionel Dahmer it was acceptable, started to highly bother her. This started arguments between the two. In such situations, Joyce would often leave the house, and "go to a nearby park, where she sat on a bench, wrapped in her coat, all alone in the snow, until I came for her, tugged her from the bench, and walked her back to the house" (Dahmer, 1994, p. 32).

1.1 Being in the womb

According to Lionel, Joyce seems to be in a constant state of sadness, and as well she constantly needed love reassurance, which Lionel expressed it through hard work so she can satisfy all her needs and as well their future together. Joyce started to have muscle spasms due to their living conditions. Two months before Jeff's birth, the pair moved to Lionel's parents' house, where Joyce developed a form of rigidity, and the muscle spasms became so severe that she was not be able to move and started to tremble. These seizures, which according to the doctor did not have anything to do with her physical state but rather with her mental state, manifested in a way that "her jaw would jerk to right, her eyes would bulge like a frightened animal, and she would begin to salivate, literally frothing at the mouth" (Dahmer, 1994, p. 34). During the seizures, Lionel and his parents, accompanied by a doctor which gave Joyce barbiturates, phenobarbital and morphine injections to relax her, would help her walk around the house. Over time she just became more irritated, tense and angry with others (Dahmer, 1994, p. 34).

During the pregnancy, Lionel was not very much present with Joyce, in fact she spent much time by herself, or with Lionel's parents.

During this time Lionel was a graduate student in the Master Program for analytical chemistry at Marquette University, and he was as well working as a graduate assistant. Joyce wanted to feel better and she sometimes took up to twenty-six pills a day, but it did not seem to help her with neither her physical pain, or with her emotional distress (Dahmer, 1994, p. 36).

1.2 Early childhood

When Jeffrey was born, he had a minor leg deformity, for which he had to wear a cast. Joyce seems to be happy again, but only for a short time due to the uncomfortable after-pregnancy symptoms. The small space they had remained in the Lionel's mother house, started fights within the family. Joyce had an alcoholic father which gave her a hard time. She never emotionally opened to Lionel, and he often retreated to his laboratory when in her rage state. Joyce remained often alone.

In the time when Jeffrey was only four months, Lionel and Joyce moved to the east side of Milwaukee. Jeffrey behaved normal for his age and he was very happy according to Lionel. He used to go for walks with his mother, which was adapting to her role of both mother and wife (Dahmer, 1994, p. 41).

Jeffrey played with "stuffed toys, bunnies and dogs, with wooden blocks that he loved to stack carefully and then push over with a sudden, powerful thrust" (Dahmer, 1994, p. 43), he also used to play a lot a game called "spider walker". Once while playing it, he hit his chin. He started to shake and hyperventilate of fright. In autumn he would gather leaves and "tear them fiercely" and when questioned about his behaviour he would answer with a smile on his face "Ruputa leaves", which means to rip leaves (Dahmer, 1994, p. 43).

In September 1962, Lionel Dahmer got a new job at the graduate assistantship in the Ph.D. program at Iowa State University, so the family moved to the campus in a smaller house than they used to live in. Joyce's emotional state began to deteriorate when she started to have a recurrent dream about a bear chasing her, which again started arguments in the family. During the same time Jeffrey caught different kinds of infections, which made him cry and therefore more irritable to the mother. Few injections he has received at the University solved this problem (Dahmer, 1994, p. 45).

As described by his father, Jeffrey was a happy kid. He was often taken to the Zoo, bicycle rides, parades and festivals, he had a swing and a sandbox built especially for him to use in the backyard. At the arrival of the father home, Jeffrey would rush and jump into his arms. He liked to play and to be read before bed time (Dahmer, 1994, p. 46).

In the second chapter of the book wrote by Jeffrey's father, he describes how he developed an obsession with fire, of which his father had no clue of, until one day Lionel almost burned down the neighbour's garage. His father than lectured him about the dangers that fire can bring. Lionel blames himself for not being able to sense when his son's obsession started to develop (Dahmer, 1994, p. 49-52).

1.3 Abnormal interests and behaviours

One day Lionel sensed a terrible smell coming from the basement. He found a large pile of white, dry, fleshless bones of rodents, which were eaten by civets, from where the smell came from. When going back up, Lionel set the bucket down. He found Jeffrey playing with the pile of bones, as he picked some up and then let them fall. The sound the bones made fascinated him: "Like fiddlesticks" he said (Dahmer, 1994, p. 53).

Other behaviours that Lionel observed, was when Jeffrey was only four years old, he asked what would happen if somebody would cut through his belly button, or when he was six, he used to break windows in abandoned buildings, when fishing, he used to stare at the gutted fish. Thinking of these, left Lionel Dahmer with constant feelings and thoughts of guilt and made him wonder if it was only curiosity, or the beginning of his son's becoming a serial killer (Dahmer, 1994, p. 54).

As Jeffrey grew and got older, his father noticed that he didn't like games which involve physical contact, but instead he liked games with highly defined rules and repetition, based on stalking and concealment, such as hide-and-sick, kick the can and ghost in the graveyard. Lionel became more and more absorbed into his job, so he only went home to eat. At these times, Jeff was hiding behind a tree or in the bushes observing (Dahmer, 1994, p. 58-59).

In 1954, Jeffrey Dahmer was diagnosed with double hernia. When he woke up from the anaesthetics, he suffered from such terrible pain, that he asked his mother if the doctors cut his penis off. His recovery was very slow (Dahmer, 1994, p. 58-59).

1.4 School time – Social anxiety or antisocial behaviour?

In October 1966, the Dahmer family moved to Ohio, as Lionel found a job there. Joyce was again pregnant, experiencing the same symptoms as in the pregnancy with Jeffrey, again taking pills against all sorts of pains, while Lionel spent most of his time at work, and Jeffrey just started first grade at Hazel Harvey Elementary School in Doylestown. In the first day of school, Jeffrey was frightened. He had a fear that other people want to harm him, which made him unsocial, distant, and he became shy over time. Jeffrey did all the assignments he was asked to do, more like a task he had to do than a task he was interested in or a task he wanted to do. He was always polite. In the breaks, Jeffrey did nothing, just kept his distance from other kids (Dahmer, 1994, p. 62-63).

When Jeffrey was seven years old, the family, which had now one member more, David, moved again, to Barberton. David kept Joyce and Lionel up all night, which made them both irritated and created arguments between them, but not the type of arguments in which they would throw stuff around and yell at each other, instead they would both retreat. Due to this, Lionel did not have so much time to attend worship services with Jeffrey anymore, but instead he found a way to combine his duties, which were all left on him after Joyce became severely depressed, that she did not get off the bed, with having fun with Jeffrey. They would often walk two miles together with Jeffrey's dog, Frisky, to a farm to buy eggs and then cook breakfast for all. And every Saturday, Lionel took Jeffrey for chocolate ice cream sodas, which was a habit of them both since Iowa (Dahmer, 1994, p. 68-69).

Not long after they moved into their new home, Jeffrey made acquaintances with the neighbour's boy, Lee, which lived behind the house where Jeffrey lived. In October they went together trick or treating, both dressed as devils (Dahmer, 1994, p. 70).

When Jeff was in third grade, he reached out and developed a kind of relationship to an assistant teacher. When asked why her, he answered with no emotions: "Because she was nice to me, I guess". Jeffrey gave her a bowl of tadpoles, which he caught in a stream in the field behind U. L. Light School, where he plays basketball with his father and his dog every Saturday. He committed his first act of violence when he found out that the assistant teacher gave the same tadpoles to Lee, so he went to pour motor oil in the water where the tadpoles were and killed them (Dahmer, 1994, p. 71-72).

Lionel Dahmer mentions that according to a psychiatric evaluation which he later read, Jeffrey had his first sexual phantasy when he was about fourteen, but he claims that he has seen changes in his son way before he was fourteen, and right before he talked about his own sexual fantasies and that his first one was when he was ten years old. In the third chapter of the book Lionel wrote, he talks about how Jeffrey changed once he became a teenager. The loose boy was replaced by "a strangely rigid and inflexible figure", which was continuously tense, with his body very straight, poker face, and when he walked, it looked like he did not bend his knees. When approached by other people he would not know what to do, he would freeze (Dahmer, 1994, p.84).

Jeffrey became lonelier day by day. His father introduced him to different kinds of activities, which he was very interested in at the beginning, but then quickly lose interest. Jeffrey developed his own interests, which his father only found out about later in the trial. As mentioned above, he was fascinated by bones, which turned into an obsession during Jeff's teenage years. He used to go by bike to get animal remains and he would take the flesh off the bones, and he even put a dog's head on a stick, and he would bring them to the "cemetery" on a small mounted area on a neighbour's property, which he created (Dahmer, 1994, p. 75-80). By the time he was fifteen, "bizarre notions of death and dismemberment became sexually charged, sexually driven, sexually satisfied" (Dahmer, 1994, p.84).

Jeffrey as described by his father, had no friendships, had no future planes, he did what he was asked to do in school with no interest, he never showed more signs of anger than raising his voice, he never argued, but he also did not agree with anything, he was like nothing mattered to him. After graduating, he became alcoholic (Dahmer, 1994, p.81-83).

Joyce was admitted into a psychiatric hospital in the summer of 1970. Six years later the marriage between Lionel and Joyce began to deteriorate due to the huge number of arguments. Jeffrey's brother, Dave observed Jeff slapping trees with branches when their parents argued. In the senior year of

Jeffrey, his dad suggested him ideas of where he could go to college, but he refused them all indirectly. Over time, they became very distant from each other (Dahmer, 1994, p.89).

1.5 The beginning of Jeffrey's alcoholism

In August 1977, Joyce divorced from Lionel and fought for the custody of Dave, which she was granted, since Jeffrey was already eighteen there was no need to fight for custody of him, but he continued to live with his mother and his brother in the same house, while Lionel came to visit every weekend. Normally he would call before, but suddenly those calls were not answered anymore, so when Lionel got to the house, all that Jeffrey kept telling him was that they moved out, nothing more. In the house there were some acquaintances of Jeffrey which Lionel kicked them all out and inspected the house, in which he found a pentagram drawn with chalk on the coffee table, only to later find out that Jeffrey wanted to contact the dead. Lionel and his new girlfriend, Shari, moved in the house with Jeffrey so he is not alone. Not long after Shari discovered that Jeffrey developed an alcohol problem. Within two weeks of the drinking episode, Shari realized that two of her rings are missing one after the other, so since she was sure she didn't lose a second one, she declared them stolen. Since there were no signs of forced entry in the house, the fault fell on a friend of Jeffrey which had access to the house. The police confirmed to Shari that this friend of Jeffrey was at fault, but also that Jeffrey knew about it. When confronted by his father and stepmother, Jeffrey feeling insulted, denied he was involved or knew anything (Dahmer, 1994, p.90-97).

As Lionel states in the last two chapters, his son had always this blank look, wall, emotionless face. As he found out later that his son has a drinking problem, he thought that this is all due to the drinking, but during the trial he learned that during this time Jeffrey was re-watching in his head his first murder which he committed in the summer of 1978, when he was only eighteen years old. Lionel finally managed to convince Jeffrey to go to university. In September 1978 Lionel and Shari drove Jeffrey to Columbus campus of Ohio State. Jeffrey packed a snakeskin he got from Boy Scout Camp, and two pictures of his dog (Dahmer, 1994, p.98-100).

After just a quarter in university, Jeffrey's grades were a disaster. His parents went to pick him up from university. Embarrassed in front of his parents, Jeffrey told his parents he had trouble waking up in the morning, thing which they later also found out from Jeffrey's roommates, additionally to the explanation that this was due to the alcohol problem Jeffrey had. He drank every day. He even went to donate blood in order to get money for alcohol. Lionel told him there are two options he has to pick now, either he finds a job, or he had to join the army. Not long after, Lionel dropped his son at the Summit Mall so he can either go to the State Employment Service or any other place that hire people, but instead he kept drinking to the point where his father told him to call him when he sobers up, because he is sick of bringing him home drunk. He never called, and when Lionel did not find him at the mall whose shops were closed, he called the police only to find out his son was in jail because of disorderly conduct and drunkenness. This was the last bit, until Lionel gave Jeffrey no choice, but drove him to the recruiting office of the U.S. Army, in January 1979. He seemed scared of how strict army life would be (Dahmer, 1994, p. 103-107).

When Jeffrey came to visit his parents from the army, he was not afraid anymore, he seemed happy. He was preparing to go to for two years to Germany with the army. In the two years, he called once or twice, and he sent only few letters, despite how many Shari sent him. When Lionel thought of him, he saw him in uniform, which represented to him his salvation, but from a sudden three months before his military service should be over, Lionel was sent a bag with Jeffrey's possessions and a letter with no explanation that he was discharged from the army. He later found out it was due to alcoholism. After a month Jeffrey called them to tell them he is working in a sandwich and pizza place called Sunshine Sub Shop, in Miami, Florida (Dahmer, 1994, p. 109-111).

As usual, the conversation between Jeff and his parents was short. One day Jeffrey called his parents to tell them he has married a woman who paid him to marry her. The final call he made, was about asking Shari for money, which she refused to give to him, but instead she bought him a plane ticket for back home. At his return, he was drunk, he was unhygienic, having unkempt grown moustache and unwashed clothes with stains, and smelling like whiskey. Once back home, he helped his parents with the housework, even when he didn't want to. One day in winter, when Lionel decided to wrap the pipes with insulation, Jeffrey insisted to wrap the pipes down in the crawl space himself:

"No, don't go down there, dad", "Let me do that" (Dahmer, 1994, p.113), only to later find out that his first victim was once stored in there. Once back home, Jeffrey started to look for a job, but two weeks after he got arrested for refusing to leave the lounge where he drank straight out of the vodka bottle and for the second time was charged with drunk and disorderly conduct, and he was then taken to Akron Correctional Facility. That did not do any good to him, but since than he hasn't stopped drinking. Lionel and Shari decided that it would be the best if Jeff would visit his grandmother in Wisconsin, a suburb of Milwaukee (Dahmer, 1994, p. 111-115).

After six years living in Milwaukee, in which time Jeffrey was working as a phlebotomist at the *Milwaukee Blood Plasma*

Centre and went for help at Alcoholics Anonymous, helped his grandmother with the shopping, gardening and any other way he could, his grandmother called his parents to tell them that Jeffrey's behaviour is concerning. They found a male manikin dressed in sports shirt and shorts in his closet. When questioned by his father about why did he do it and how, he told him that he liked the clothes on the manikin, and that he had taken down the torso apart in the middle an placed the two pieces in a shopping bag and went out of the store. Lionel insisted that Jeffrey returns the stolen items back, but apparently, they've already been thrown away. This story again made Lionel have a talk to his son about possible things he could do, and once again it ended the same way as the first one, Jeffrey's response was nothing more than maybe and forgotten, so Lionel drove him himself to Milwaukee Area Technical College, he paid the tuition. But he did not go to school, and instead he found a job with a temporary agency (Dahmer, 1994, p.
117-122).

When the grandmother called Lionel again, she reported a gun found under Jeffrey's pillow. Jeffrey tried to calm her down, explaining her that he uses this gun for a shooting range in the nearby. The gun was not a target pistol, it was a Cold Lawman .357 Magnum, with a two-and-a-half-inch barrel, so Lionel took the gun way from his son, sold it and gave the money back to

Jeffrey (Dahmer, 1994, p.122-123). One day when the grandmother was on the way down the stairs, Jeffrey told her to stop and go back up because he is naked. Later that day she saw Jeffrey again, with another very drunk man, who he casually met. He brought him in the basement telling his grandmother that he would not like it if he throws up in the house, but there the two got drunker, so Jeffrey brought him to the bus stop and put him on a bus. The man was gone, and the case was closed. Again, the grandmother reported to Jeffrey's parents, this time that there is a very strange odour in the garage, for which of course

Jeffrey had an excuse, such as he experimented with bleach and muriatic acid on chicken parts he bought from the store, or the second time this happened his excuse was that the smell comes from the cleaning products he used to clean the garage, and finally after Lionel interrogated him, he told him the "truth", that he picked up dead racoons and wanted to experiment and see what the chemicals would do (Dahmer, 1994, p.123-126).

1.6 Jeffrey's crimes

By 1988 Jeffrey Dahmer killed four men, two of them in the basement of the grandmother, was twice arrested for indecent exposure in 1982 and 1986. In 1985 in West Allis Library, a man passed him a note telling him if he wants a blowjob he should go to the men's room. This note gave him motivation to go to the bathhouses, where he knocked out men with drugs to have sex with their unresponsive bodies (Dahmer, 1994, p.131).

In 1985, Jeffrey got a job at the Ambroisa Chocolate Factory in Milwaukee, and on September 26, 1988, he moved out from his grandmother's house with the excuse that he wants to live closer to where he works. At that same time his grandmother had found a sort of Satanic altar, with griffins and black lights, to which Jeffrey's explanation was a typical one, as his was tired of explaining himself anymore. On his first day in his new apartment, he already brought a thirteen-year-old boy in his apartment, by offering him fifty dollars to pose nude, drugged him and sexually molested him. The boy left and took the police to Dahmer. He got arrested at work. Few days later Jeffrey was released with the help of his father and grandmother which paid his bail, with the condition that he moves back to his grandmother's house, and as usual having an explanation for what he has done. He moved back to his grandmother's house (Dahmer, 1994, p.131-135).

Eight months later, he had to go to the court for child molestation. His father found a small wooden box in his room, and when asked to open it Jeffrey refused. His father took a guess that in there might be pornographic magazines, but later he learned that there laid a human head inside (Dahmer, 1994, p. 147).

On May 23, 1989, the judge sentenced Jeff to five years of probation, during which he killed another human. The judge decided to send Jeffrey for a year to the House of Correction. Mr. Boyle, Jeffrey's lawyer, said that he would do all he can to grant him an early release, despite to Lionel's concerns of setting his son free while he is still an alcoholic. He has believed that all the problems he has caused are due to his alcoholism (Dahmer, 1994, p. 147).

At the end of February 1990, Jeffrey was released two months earlier from the House of Correction Milwaukee, with probation for the next few years. His probation consisted only on sometimes paying a visit to his probation officer. Jeffrey moved back to his grandmother's house in West Allis, but his grandmother became very old so eventually he had to move out (Dahmer, 1994, p.136-143). He found an apartment on North Twenty-fifth Street, number 213, which was approved by the probation officer. When his parents visited him, he presented to them how clean and neat the place is. They noticed a door between the corridor and the living room, highly secured, of course Jeffrey explained why very well as usual. Later Jeffrey had installed alarms and a camera above the door (Dahmer, 1994, p. 147).

On the Thanksgiving Day of 1990 the whole family, including Jeffrey was supposed to go celebrate at the grandmother's house, where there were no more strange odours coming from the basement since her grandson moved out. Jeffrey arrived one day late, looking very fresh, and with a new interest in aquarium fish (Dahmer, 1994, p. 136-146).

"With each mention that I or someone else in the family may drop by to pay him a visit, it twitches. With each mention of what he is doing now, of how his job is going, of what he does in his spare time-it twitches. Something in his distant, half-dead gaze says, 'If you only knew'" (Dahmer, 1994, p. 147).

On July 22, 1991, nobody in the family could reach Jeffrey, until a Milwaukee police officer picked up the phone in his apartment and told Lionel Dahmer that he will be called by a detective. The next day the police were searching the house, especially the basement of the grandmother, when they informed Lionel Dahmer, that his son was arrested for homicide (Dahmer, 1994, p. 147-159).

Mr. Boyle was the one to tell Lionel Dahmer, his son is suicidal. When Lionel met his son, Jeffrey showed no emotion and he kept saying sorry, but not looking like he meant it. Lionel was wondering what he is sorry for. For the men he killed, for his family, for both? Almost all Jeffrey's victims were poor black men. On August 28, the lawyer told Lionel that Jeffrey does not want to see them because he is embarrassed by what he has done.

By the fall of 1991, Jeffrey was known as a monster, a ghoul and a demon. He was thought to be a psychologically sadistic killer. According to Tracy Edwards, one which escaped Jeffrey Dahmer stated that Jeffrey wanted to eat his heart. Pat Synder, a former Ohio acquaintance of Lionel Dahmer, which did not meet the Dahmer's more than three times for very short time, he accused Shari being the evil stepmother. Another person who refused to give his identity, "Nick", claimed he was in a relationship with Jeffrey since 1985, and stated that he was jealous, but not violent, and after they two became close Jeffrey told him that "Lionel sexually abused him in childhood", thing Lionel claims not to be true. As soon as Jeffrey heard the statement of this person, he filed a legal affidavit denying the sayings of "Nick" (Dahmer, 1994, p. 179-203).

Jeffrey Dahmer's trial began on January 30, 1992. Around the building and in the courtroom, there were highly security measures taken, there were metal detectors at the entrance of the courtroom, police dogs, and an eight-foot bulletproof glass for Jeffrey. His parents were warned not to show up because of the danger, but Lionel did not want Jeffrey to feel abandoned. At the trial nobody wanted to be near them. The purpose of the trial was to declare whether Jeffrey was insane when he committed the murders. Nothing from the crimes Jeffrey has committed was left out at the trial, murder, evisceration, cannibalism and necrophilia (Dahmer, 1994, p. 107-210).

Steven Tuomi, a twenty-five years old cook, met Jeffrey Dahmer in front of a club, and then left together to the Ambassador Hotel, where both had drinks, and the next morning Jeffrey woke up next to the bruised, dead body of Tuomi. Jeffrey remembered and confessed to the police everything he had done, but he has no memory of what happened at the Ambassador Hotel with Tuomi, he stated that he probably beaten him to death. Another victim was Hicks. While driving his mother's car, Jeffrey saw and was attracted to Hicks who was naked to the waist. He took him to the house of Bath Road, where he used to live with his mother, Joyce, he served him with beer and weed, but when Hicks wanted to leave Jeffrey murdered him (Dahmer, 1994, p. 214-216). "This dread of people leaving him had been the root of more than one of Jeff's murders. In general, Jeff had simply wanted to "keep" people permanently", "it was a mania that had begun with fantasies of unmoving bodies" (Dahmer, 1994, p. 216). The psychiatry testimony reviled nothing unsurprising, but the theme of control, which was a huge theme in one of Jeffrey's big fantasies as well. He wanted absolute control over the people (Dahmer, 1994, p. 219).

1.7 **Sexual fantasies**

The first time Jeffrey had the occasion to a sexual encounter he carried a baseball bat with him to knock him out and "lay" with him. Drugging his victims was only the beginning of his wish of fulfilling his sexual desires and attaining full control over people, eventually people would wake up. Dahmer wanted to create a sex zombie, which he would be able to fully control. He experimented on people while they were still alive, by lobotomizing them with muriatic acid. Usually this kills people instantly, but there was one which survived full two days (Dahmer, 1994, p. 214-221).

> "He began to concentrate on the dead. He looked through the obituary columns, found a funeral notice of an eighteen-year-old boy, and plotted to dig up the corpse and bring it home so that he could enjoy the level of control which only could be gotten from the dead" (Dahmer, 1994, p. 220).

2. **Necrophilia**

The term "necrophilia" was formed from the Greek word "nekros", which means dead body, and the word "philia", which means both love and friendship. Necrophilia is a rare sexual disorder, in which one is attracted, and gets sexual gratification from having sexual intercourse with a dead body (Aggrawal, 2016, p.1).

It appears that neither psychosis, nor mental retardation, nor sadism are inherent in necrophilia. The most common reason to be a necrophiliac is to not be rejected and to have complete control over someone's body. Most necrophiliacs would choose and occupation where they can easily get in contact with dead bodies (Rosman & Resnick, 1989, p.153). Recently necrophilia has been often associated with other types of paraphilias such as sadism, cannibalism, consuming fresh meat, or for spiritual purposes, vampirism, which by definition is drinking blood from a person or animal, necrophagia, is eating flesh of the dead, necropedophilia, sexual attraction or interaction to children's corpses, and necrozoophilia or necrobestiality, the sexual attraction to the corpses of or killings of animals (Aggrawal, 2016, p.1).

2.1 Necrophilia in history

Necrophilia is known since ancient times. It is probably as old as civilization itself, and it was present in many different cultures, but mainly dominant in ancient Egypt. One story most people heard of is back in the times when people died in foreign countries, their bodies were transported on water back to their homeland. It is believed that during the transportation of the bodies on water, sailors committed acts of necrophilia due to their loneliness and lack of witnesses (Aggrawal, 2016, p.2).

Egyptians believed that even after death one still owns his sexual powers, like Osiris, the king of death still had them, so many embalmers, abused the dead bodies of beautiful women. This is how Egyptians began to mummify the dead (Manniche, 2009, p.28-29). It is believed that to prevent people to commit acts of necrophilia, the "curse of pharaoh's tomb" myth was invented, in other countries they buried the bodies very deep or in granite and marble, or even burn them (Aggrawal, 2016, p.6). Achilles killed Penthesilea, an Amazonian Queen, in the Trojan War, but after removing her helmet, he fell in love with her and has sexual intercourse with her body (Aggrawal, 2016, p.5). Periander (625–585 B.C.), the second tyrant of Corinth, Greece, he murdered his wife Melissa, and then had sexual intercourse with her dead body (Aggrawal, 2016, p.6). Victor Ardisson, a mortician of Le Muy, a tiny town in France, and known as the "busiest" necrophile in history, for having sexual intercourse with approximately one hundred dead bodies. He was very upset that the bodies did not respond when he talked to them (Aggrawal, 2016, p.9).

2.2 Diagnosis, types and classification of necrophilia

In DSM V, necrophilia can be found under the code of 302.9. Paraphilias Otherwise Specified (American Psychiatric

Association, 2013). In ICD 10, necrophilia can be found under the code F65.9. Paraphilia, unspecified. In ICD 9, volume 2, necrophilia can be found under 302.9 Sexual deviation, as 302.89 Necrophilia (World Health Organization, 1992).

According to (Rosman & Rechnick), there are two types of necrophilia, genuine necrophilia and pseudonecrophilia.

Genuine necrophilia is a persistent attraction to corpses manifested through fantasies and necrophiliac acts (Rosman & Resnick, 1989, p.154).

- *Necrophiliac homicide*: Necrophiliac homicide can be defined as committing a murder in order to get a corpse for sexual pleasure (Rosman & Resnick, 1989, p.154).
- *"Regular" necrophilia*: "Regular" necrophilia is the use of already dead bodies for sexual pleasure (Rosman & Resnick, 1989, p.154).
- *Necrophiliac fantasy*: Necrophiliac fantasies are sexual fantasies that involve a dead body without acting on it (Rosman & Resnick, 1989, p.154).

Pseudonecrophilia is an impermanent form of attraction to corpses, where the corpse is not the main object to satisfy one's sexual needs (Rosman & Resnick, 1989, p.154).

Concerning the classification, it can be stated that necrophilia seems to be easy to classify but there are many types of necrophiliac behaviours that have been discovered, ranging from fantasizing to committing murder for a dead body.

- *Class I – The role players*: These are people who get aroused by their partner pretending to be dead during the sexual act, but never have sex with a corpse (Aggrawal, 2016, p.47-48).
- *Class II – Romantic necrophiliacs*: These are people who cannot get over the death of a loved one (Aggrawal, 2016, p.48-51).
- *Class III – Necrophiliac fantasizers*: People who fantasize and get aroused by corpses, but never engage in any necrophiliac activity, but only in activities that allow them to easier see corpses (Aggrawal, 2016, p.51-55).
- *Class IV – Tactile necrophiles*: People which achieve an orgasm by touching parts of a dead body such as genitals, or licking breasts. They seek out jobs that can give them access to corpses (Aggrawal, 2016, p.56-59).
- *Class V – Fetishistic necrophiliacs*: These people don't have sexual contact with dead bodies but if they have the chance, they might keep some part of the body for continuous erotic stimulation (Aggrawal, 2016, p.59-63).
- *Class VI – Necromutilomaniacs*: People who enjoy masturbating while mutilating a dead body.

Necrophagy, eating parts of a corpse and getting sexual pleasure, can be found under the same classification (Aggrawal, 2016, p.63-66).

- *Class VII – Opportunistic necrophiliacs*: People who engage in normal sexual activities but if they have the opportunity they would engage in a sexual activity with a corpse (Aggrawal, 2016, p.67-69).
- *Class VIII – Regular necrophiliacs*: The "classical" necrophiliacs who prefere to have sex with the dead instead of the living. They are likely to steal dead bodies from graveyards or morgues (Aggrawal, 2016, p.69-73).
- *Class IX – Homicidal necrophiliacs*: Also known as lust murders. The most dangerous type of necrophiliacs. They murder so they can have sex with a corpse (Aggrawal, 2016, p.73-84).
- *Class X – Exclusive necrophiliacs*: This is the rarest subtype of necrophilia.

These are people who psychologically and physiologically can't engage in a sexual activity with a living person, but only with a dead person (Aggrawal, 2016, p.8).

2.3 Etiology

Considering the wide spectrum of necrophiliacs, the etiology is not yet clear. There are many aspects that play a role in one becoming a necrophiliac. A single definition will not be enough to explain everyone's behaviour. So in this chapter all etiological theories proposed so far will be presented.

The following approaches are connected to biological factors:

- *Trauma*: Head injury resulting with a concussion may be a possible cause of necrophilia. Several examples can support this statement, such as Joseph Vacher, which after he shot himself in the head and survived started showing necrophiliac tendencies, John Reginald Halliday Christie, which also started showing necrophiliac tendencies after he was hit by a car, and diagnosed with a major injury to the head, collarbone and knee (Aggrawal, 2016, p.25).
- *Sexual Inadequacy*: Sexual inadequacy can intensify the interest in corpses. Necrophiles are known to be impotent to living women, because of fear to perform. This anxiety is usually due to a psychological problem. In front of a lifeless person whether one can perform or not, is not important anymore, so this fear is not present anymore (Aggrawal, 2016, p.25).

- *Alcoholism*: Many necrophiliacs were under the influence of alcohol when acted upon their fantasies. The most known case is of Jeffrey Dahmer, which tended to become hostile and aggressive while drinking alcohol, as well he committed most of his murders under the influence of alcohol (Aggrawal, 2016, p.28).

- *Drugs*: Cocaine is very well known and associated with criminal behaviour. The case of a man who killed twice for sexual pleasure in 2004, under the influence of alcohol, cocaine and crack, was the first time to associate the use of drugs with necrophiliac acts. Another case in which necrophilia was associated with drug use was a twenty-six-year-old African-American, which from early adolescence had used alcohol, opiates, sedative-hypnotics, amphetamine, cannabis, hallucinogens, and phencyclidine, killed his wife and had sexual intercourse with her dead body (Aggrawal, 2016, p.28-29).

- *Temporal lobe anomalies*: Temporal lobe anomalies, which can derive from excessive drinking, are associated with many of the paraphilias.

Psychoanalysis provides its own approach to necrophilia; in the following, outstanding approaches are presented:

- *Unconscious suppressed hostility*: There is an unconscious suppressed hostility toward parental figures and sadistic

impulses to explore the mother's body. In this theory
necrophilia develops from hate towards the mother
(Aggrawal, 2016, p.32).

- *Wanting full control*: Most necrophiliacs enjoy having
complete power and control over one, which is only possible
only if their victims are dead (Aggrawal, 2016, p.33).
- *Castration anxiety*: Castration anxiety, feelings of male
inadequacy, and fear of women may be also a factor that
influences necrophilia. In this case the person wants to prove
his strength by inflicting humiliation on a helpless victim
(Aggrawal, 2016, p.35).
- *Oral fixation*: The case of a man who loved to perform a
fellatio on living men, so he can satisfy his pleasure, until he
got punched by one. Thereafter he began killing them so
they would not get in the way during the process. This desire
relates to the oral stage of the sexual development stages.
When the one becomes orally fixated it results in fellatio in
adult life (Aggrawal, 2016, p.35).
- Attitude towards sex: Many parents have taught their
children, maybe still do, that sex is dirty and unnatural, which
may influence one to believe that sex with dead bodies is not
real sex (Aggrawal, 2016, p.36).
- Dalmau's theory: Dalmau modified Freud's theory of Oedipus
complex stating that the theory was created in a time when
the father was the authority figure in family. According to

Dalmau, the father still remains the main enemy for a male child, but the mother will be eventually seen as a frustrating figure, which will influence the phallic sadistic drives with feelings of wanting to murder and rape the mother. This is the core of necrophilia, male homosexuality and impotence (Aggrawal, 2016, p.36).

In some cases, acting on necrophiliac fantasies may be due to the melancholia caused by the loss of a loved one, and the desire to reconnect, or be one more time with them. Also, there are cases of necrophilia caused by rejection (Aggrawal, 2016, p.37).

3. Psychosexual development of Jeffrey Dahmer according to Freud

3.1 Dahmer's broken home

After the divorce of Jeffrey Dahmer's parents, he was left in the custody of his mother, which in the end she also has abandoned Jeffrey, so he moved to his grandmother's house (Tithecott, 1999, p.45). Jeffrey's homosexuality is associated with his father's absence, and once with that, the absence of obeying laws and rules, and the feminine dominance in his life, trying to be "the mamma's boy", which created the "homosexual mass murderer" (Tithecott, 1999, p. 46).

Serial killers usually come from broken homes, separated or divorced parents, in which the father is absent most of the time, and the feminine dominance takes the lead, and or not enough consistent discipline (Tithecott, 1999, p.45).

"The individual growing up in a female-dominated family is commonly perceived as an unpredictable figure whose actions appear motiveless" (Tithecott, 1999, p.45).

The blame is usually given to the women, to the mothers, but the fathers play a huge role in raising children as well, and they already play a big role only by being present. As with the case of Lionel Dahmer, he feels guilty he did not spend much time with Jeffrey, and wonders if this would have been the case, if anything would have been different (Tithecott, 1999, p.45-46).

3.2 Psychosexual development according to Freud

Sigmund Freud, the 'father' of the psychosexual development theory, believed that how parents handled their child's sexual and aggressive behaviours in the first years If life, will have a very huge impact on the child's personality later in life (Dragic, 2018, p.12). The psychosexual development consists of five stages (see table).

FREUD'S STAGES OF PSYCHOSEXUAL DEVELOPMENT

Stage	Approximate Ages	Erotic Focus	Key Tasks and Experiences
Oral	0–1	Mouth (sucking, biting)	Weaning (from breast or bottle)
Anal	1-3	Anus (expelling or retaining feces)	Toilet training
Phallic	3-6	Genitals (sexuality explored)	Identifying with adult role models; coping with Oedipal crisis
Latency	6–12	None (sexuality refined)	Expanding social contacts
Genital	Puberty onward	Genitals (being sexually intimate)	Establishing intimate relationships; contributing to society through working

oral-dependent personality: a passive person who takes more than he gives
oral-aggressive personality: a hostile vocal person who is also exploitative.
anal-expulsive personality: a disorderly, messy person(Oscar of "The Odd Couple").
anal-retentive personality: a stingy, compulsive "neatnick"(Felix of "The Odd Couple").
phallic-personality: a person who is vain, narcissistic, & exhibitionistic.

("Revision Guide: Development Psychology")

During the childhood, one comes across all stages. Depending on if the parents permit too much, or too little gratification of the child's needs, decides on the outcome of the child's personality (Dragic, 2018, p.12). Across these stages, one will encounter conflicts. If these conflicts cannot be resolved at the appropriate stage, fixations occur.

Three other parts of the personality, the id, the ego and the superego, become involved during these five stages. The id is the source of the basic biological needs. The ego is our consciousness, or rational impulses, which control the id, for us to behave appropriately at the right times. The super ego, which is our conscience, develops between the ages of three to six, though the interaction with the parents. The relationship between these three parts of the personality until the age of six to seven, can determine one's basic personality (Dragic, 2018, p.12)

3.2.1 Oral stage

Oral stage is first in the theory of psychosexual development of Freud. This stage occurs from birth to the age of one year. In this stage babies focus their libidinal pleasure on feeding, which it is a source of gratification, coming mostly from the mother. When the babies receive enough oral stimulation during this stage, it allows them to develop trust in the primary caregiver (Maltby, Day, & Macaskill, 2011, p. 26).

> "The infant whose needs are met develops this basic trust in others, while the child whose needs are not met develops a sense of mistrust" (Maltby, Day, & Macaskill, 2011, p. 26).

In the case where the baby receives under or over stimulation, which is known as a failure of the stage, fixation can occur in later adult life. This can be later observed in the personality and behaviour of the affected adults, which commonly is shown through an excessive oral stimulation such as smoking, drinking, chewing gum, or excessive eating (Maltby, Day, & Macaskill, 2011, p. 27).

Joyce had a hard time bonding and breast-feeding Jeffrey as a baby due to her mental problems, which might have led to the oral fixation of Jeffrey, the alcohol abuse. This is known as under-indulgence, which can lead to oral aggressive personality, in which the person affected is exploiting others, trying to get as much as possible from them. In an extreme case these people show sadistic behaviour and dominance (Maltby, Day, & Macaskill, 2011, p. 27).

3.2.2 Anal stage

The second psychosexual stage by Freud, which follows the oral stage, occurs from the ages of eighteen months to the age of three. In this stage the child receives the pleasure from bowel movements, and in the same time the toilet training begins. Rewarding is important when the child has gained control of their bladder and bowel. The child may resist the toilet training if the parents are too demanding, which later can make the child rebel authority figures. When the toilet training hasn't been done properly, fixation on the anal stage occurs, resulting into anal retentive or anal expulsive personality (Maltby, Day, & Macaskill, 2011, pp. 27-28).

Anal retentive personality is characterized by stubbornness, stinginess and the individual may show hoarding tendencies for delaying the gratification. Anal expulsive personality is characterized by being disorganized and not respecting the rules (Maltby, Day, & Macaskill, 2011, pg. 28).

As described in the first chapter, before the age of four Jeffrey Dahmer had a strong fascination for bones, but this fascination never became anal expulsive or anal retentive.

3.2.3 Phallic stage – Failed Oedipus complex

The phallic stage, which focuses on the genital area, occurs between the ages of three to five, in which gratification is obtained through masturbation. In this stage what is known as the penis envy and castration anxiety occurs in children. The penis envy according to Freud, is the jealousy of a girl for not having a penis, and the wish of the girls to have one. Castration anxiety is shown by the boys, with the fear of losing their penis as a response to the penis envy (Maltby, Day, & Macaskill, 2011, p. 28).

During the phallic stage the child-parent relationship becomes one in which the boys think of the mothers as sexual objects, so the father becomes an opponent, which the boy fears due to the recognition of the father as being a powerful, threatening figure, with the power to castrate the boy (Maltby, Day, & Macaskill, 2011, p. 28). This is known as Oedipus complex.

"The boy is thus trapped between his desire for his mother and his fear of his father" (Maltby, Day, & Macaskill, 2011, p. 28).

This causes anxiety, and in order to resolve this problem, the boy tries to become more like his father, which will be the core of the child's superego (Maltby, Day, & Macaskill, 2011, p. 28).

Failing this stage for boys results in sexual identity problems, difficulty to form relationships (Sharf, 2012, p.38) and the man developing female characteristics and a possible attraction to males, known as homosexuality, and as Freud calls it the unsatisfactory resolution of the phallic stage. As well later in the adulthood, the man may search to fulfil his sexual desires that were denied to him during the childhood (Maltby, Day, & Macaskill, 2011, p. 28).

Jeffrey Dahmer has formed a fixation at this stage. He has failed the Oedipus complex. Joyce had a difficult time bonding with Jeffrey, and after a while she took his brother and abandoned him. Jeffrey could not associate the pleasure with his mom, so instead he was focused on getting this pleasure from fully controlling other people, so they cannot abandon him either, which resulted in Jeffrey killing them for fulfilling this need.

3.2.4 Latent stage

The latency stage happens between the age of five to twelve. During this time the child is focusing on forming a social life and on learning. The peer group interaction during this stage is mostly with the same-sex children. Identification with the father becomes identification with same-sexed individuals. Children build up defence mechanisms to cope with the anxiety caused by the conflicts between the id, ego and superego (Maltby, Day, & Macaskill, 2011, pp. 28-29).

According to Freud there were eleven main defence mechanisms, starting with the first, repression, denial, projection, reaction formation, rationalization, conversation reaction, phobic avoidance, displacement, regression, isolation and undoing (Maltby, Day, & Macaskill, 2011, p. 29).

As Jeffrey Dahmer was stuck in the phallic stage, and wasn't able to identify with his father, he has never developed his superego properly, and has never learned to create healthy relationships with his peers. As he began to go to school, he was very anxious and became avoidant.

3.2.5 Genital stage

The last stage of Freud's psychosexual development stages, takes place between the age of twelve till eighteen years or older. The sexual energy is again present, and as mentioned before, in normal development this is fulfilled with the opposite sex. In the case of a failed Oedipus complex, the person does not cope well with the sexual energy during this stage, especially when the first three most important stages, oral, anal and phallic stages, are not fulfilled, which in case of Jeffrey Dahmer they were not (Maltby, Day, & Macaskill, 2011, p.29). During this stage Jeffrey was already lonely; a little later he became an alcoholic and then joined the army in order to suppress his sexual desires. He has failed to do so, so he remained at associating pleasure with fully controlling a person, which resulted in their death.

4. Psychodynamic perspective on personality

"Personality is the complex organisation of cognitions,
affects, and behaviours that gives direction and pattern
(coherence) to the person's life. Like the body,
personality consists of both structures and processes,
and reflects both nature (genes) and nurture
(experience). In addition, personality includes the
effects of the past, including memories of the past, as
well as constructions of the present and future"
(Mischel, Shoda, & Ayduk, 2008, p.3).
According to Freud, personality problems can be due to the
castration anxiety, as well memories from previous stages
(Sharf, 2012, p.38).

4.1 Development of personality according to Freud

Freud holds that the psychic apparatus consists of three
instances, the Id, the Ego and the Super-Ego. Famously,
these instances can be depicted in the iceberg model:

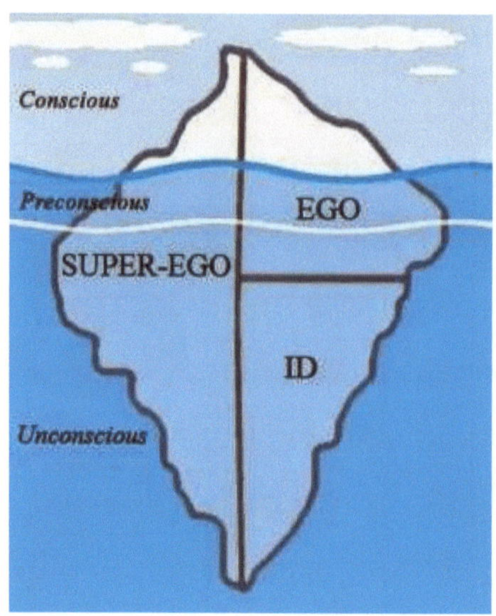

The psychic apparatus – Freud

(Mcleod, 2018)

The Id is known as the primary process. The infant is all Id from birth. The Id is the centre of pleasure, driven by unconsciousness. In a baby the centre of the pleasure is the nipple of the mother. The baby seeks the nipple of the mother when hungry, in order to satisfy his or her needs. For adults the Id is seen in wishful fantasies that come from the unconscious, such as dreams. The ego must make the difference between fantasy and reality (Sharf, 2012, p.34-35).

The Ego, known as the secondary process, has the function to set a balance between a person's desires and the world around. For example, a baby learns to ask for food instead of crying when his or her needs are not met. It is the function of the ego to help us think logically and develop ways to satisfy our needs (Sharf, 2012, p.35).

The Superego represents parental values and society standards. It is responsible to form a moral code, so one can tell good from bad. The role of the superego is to suppress any id desires unaccepted by the society, and to force the ego to become more morally focused rather than realistic (Sharf, 2012, p.35).

4.2 Types of anxieties resulting from inner-psychic conflicts

When conflicts between the three main structures of personality arise, it will result in anxiety (Sharf, 2012, p.35).

- *Reality anxiety*: Fear of the external world in an appropriate situation, such as keeping distance from a person we may find threatening (Sharf, 2012, p.35).
- *Neurotic anxiety*: Neurotic anxiety, the one Jeffrey indeed suffered of, is the fear of not being able to control fantasies and desires driven by the id, which may result in punishment from parental or authority figures (Sharf, 2012, p.35).
- *Moral anxiety*: Is the fear of violating the standards of parents or society, and it triggers the defense mechanisms (Sharf, 2012, p.35).

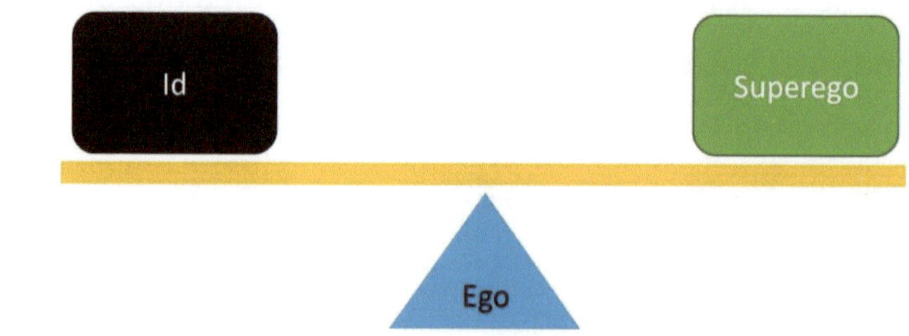

("Freudian Psychoanalysis", 2018)

The development of one's personality, the id, ego and superego, are determined by how well the first five years of the psychosexual development goes (Sharf, 2012, p.37). Conflicts between these three structures and out attempts to balance what each of them wants determine how we act and approach the world.

5. Conclusion

Since Jeffrey Dahmer had many diagnoses, he is one of the most suitable serial killers for purpose of psychoanalysis. During his active years, Jeffrey Dahmer killed seventeen young men in the area of Milwaukee, mutilated and perpetrated sexual acts to their bodies, and he even ate different body parts of his victims.

Before his trial, his mental condition was questioned, whether he was mentally fit to stand trial, or whether he should be committed to a mental hospital. It was not possible to comprehend how someone who could be capable of perpetrating such heinous offenses could be mentally suitable to stand trial. The definition of legal insanity and sanity differ significantly from the daily description; thus, it would have been the work of the forensic psychologists to make the determination.

He was deemed fit to stand trial legally since he knew wrong from right evidenced by the fact that he had tried covering up his offenses, which can be also determined by his psychoanalysis which strongly suggests that Jeffrey suffered of neurotic anxiety. He had a strong Id, the unconscious component of personality, the source of pleasure, which drove him to commit the crimes, and a very small super ego, the component formed by the moral standards we learn from our parents, so he could not suppress his desires, and let himself be fully controlled by the Id.

The whole scope of Jeffery's profile established factors that continue to be assessed in serial killers for both treatment and study. The psychodynamic aspects shed light onto areas of sadism, cannibalism and necrophilia. His abnormal development, caused by the relationship with his parents mainly, most likely was the reason he developed compulsions to perform such gruesome criminal acts.

Bibliography

Aggrawal, A. (2016). *Necrophilia: Forensic and Medico-legal Aspects*. CRC Press.

American Psychiatric Association (2013). Paraphilic Disorders. In *Diagnostic and statistical manual of mental disorders* (5th ed.).

Dahmer, L. (1994). *A father's story*. New York: W. Morrow.

Dragic, I., (2018, November). *Developmental Psychology. Lecture presented at Developmental Psychology Lecture in Sigmund Freud Private University*. Vienna: Unpublished lecture notes.

Freudian Psychoanalysis (2018, May 31). Retrieved from https://www.psychologyexams.com/2018/04/25/freudian-psychoanalysis/

Maltby, J., Day, L., & Macaskill, A. (2011). *Personality, individual differences and intelligence*. M xico: Pearson ducaci n.

Manniche, L. (2009). *Sexual life in ancient Egypt*. London: Kegan Paul.

Mcleod, S. (2018, April 5). *What are the most interesting ideas of Sigmund Freud?* Retrieved from https://www.simplypsychology.org/SigmundFreud.html

Mischel, W., Shoda, Y., & Ayduk, O. (2008). *Introduction to personality: toward an integrative science of the person*. Hoboken (Nueva Jersey): John Wiley & Sons.

Revision Guide: *Development Psychology*. (2006, May). Retrieved July 3, 2019, from http://studyguideappsych.blogspot.com/

Rosman, J. P., & Resnick, P. J. (1989). Sexual Attraction to Corpses: A Psychiatric Review of Necrophilia. *The Bulletin of the American Academy of Psychiatry and the Law, 17*(2), 153-163.

Sharf, R. S. (2012). *Theories of psychotherapy and counseling: concepts and cases*. Belmont, CA: Brooks/Cole.

Tithecott, R. (1999). *Of Men and Monsters: Jeffrey Dahmer and the Construction of the Serial Killer*. Wisconsin: University of Wisconsin Press.

World Health Organization. (1992). *The ICD-10 classification of mental and behavioural disorders: Clinical descriptions and diagnostic guidelines.* Geneva: World Health Organization.